[CONTEMPORARY LIVING WITH ANTIQUES]

BETA-PLUS

[CONTEMPORARY LIVING WITH ANTIQUES]

This is an InTempo by Luc Leroi project
in the Luxembourg countryside.

A Mark Mertens (am projects) interior
in a farmhouse in West Flanders.

[CONTENTS]

[FOREWORD]

The historic value of their top pieces is no longer the one thing that counts for visionary antiques dealers: the 'decorative' meaning is also of essential importance.

Valuable antique objects can give a major added value to a classical or ultramodern interior just like works of art, not due to their museological merit but due to their look, their unique patina, their testimony to a glorious past or far flung cultural origin.

This book presents dozens of examples of recently constructed or restored homes where interior designers and antiques dealers provide an eclectic whole of old and new.

Wim Pauwels
Publisher

The home office of Eddy Dankers,
with a boiserie by Axel Vervoordt.

12-13
A custom made kitchen by Mark
Mertens (Am projects) with furniture
from his Am projects collection.

A HOUSE IN THE LUXEMBOURG COUNTRYSIDE

This house was built in 2007 and is situated in the Luxembourg countryside.
The interior combines both neutral and timeless elements with some antiques, using natural and noble materials.

The house is also used as a show-room for the owners' interior design and decoration business: In Tempo by Luc Leroi.

Their philosophy lies in the creation of timeless interiors favouring materials such as natural wood, stone, lime, linen and an overarching use of artisanal work.

The stairway is simply laid with untreated wide oak boards. Metal door.

The modest entrance hall is laid with
church tiles by Dominique Desimpel.

A sofa upholstered in Libeco linen, a table de vigneron dressed with antique olive wood mortars. All the walls of the lounge and dining room are rendered in Corical lime-wash paint.

The ground floor is laid with antique Corvelyn parquet. The oak chest of drawers is simply stripped. Bespoke armchairs are upholstered in C&C Milano covers.

A view along the hall affords a full appreciation of the double exposure of the rooms in succession. Curtains in Leitner linen. An antique 19th century chandelier. An 18th century Namur wardrobe holding a collection of Chinese pots.

The kitchen is in untreated oak, with a work top in blue stone and credenza covered in red zellige tiles from Dominique Desimpel. Integrated storage cabinet and fridge in a cupboard painted the same colour as the wall.

Pantry. The storage units have been custom-made. Underfoot, checkerboard flooring in Italian marble by Dominique Desimpel.

The hall leading to the bedrooms is in rough grey oak. A Spanish console table in walnut from the 18th century. C&C Milano linen blinds.

The office has an antique pine
table and an 18th century "Os
de mouton" chair. Lighting
from S.Davidts.

The master bedroom has been rendered in white lime-wash paint. An Anker bedding bed with Libeco linen cover. Wall-lights from Galerie des lampes – Paris.

A custom-made dressing, painted white.

This bedroom is furnished with Swedish furniture from the 17th and 18th centuries.

The bathroom has a monastic feel, in oak, blue-stone and Indian schist tiles. Nautic wall-lights.

This floor is set aside as guest
suite. A pine wardrobe
originally from the Pyrenees.
A Louis XIII banquette
upholstered in white de le
Cuona linen and a coffee table
made from a walnut panel
supported on a trestle.

In Tempo by Luc Leroi
13a rue de Clairefontaine
L – 8460 Eischen
T +352 (0)48 39 68
www.intempo.lu
info@intempo.lu

A WEEKEND HOUSE
IN THE HASPENGOUW AREA

This property is located in Haspengouw, a few kilometres from Tongres, and is used as a second home. The interior is characterised by an exceptional inflow of light afforded by the double exposure from the row of main rooms in succession. The spirit of Normandy houses can be found in the design from In Tempo by Luc Leroi.

The entrance hall is laid with aged blue stone and features untreated oak joinery with a bench originally from Italy.

Modular lighting.

Spanish walnut console table decorated with various wooden
objects. The coffee table is made from an antique walnut panel.
The walls have been rendered in Corical lime-wash paint.

The lounge and dining room are laid
with antique Corvelyn parquet flooring.
Custom-made sofas and armchairs with
linen covers. Drapes in plum Libeco
linen.

"Os de mouton" chairs upholstered in Libeco linen. Double-corps dresser with sheen finish from Alsace.

The kitchen is equipped with a Lacanche range. Bespoke units in untreated oak, blue stone work top and a storage cupboard from Piedmont, Italy.

This entire floor of the house is laid with the same natural oak parquet flooring and is painted the same colour allowing a serene atmosphere to pervade. Anker bed and Lumina desk lamp.

Étagère in wide oak boards and wall-lights from S. Davidts.

Bathroom comprised of plain oak shelves on which sinks and bathroom linen are placed.

[**In Tempo by Luc Leroi**

13a rue de Clairefontaine

L – 8460 Eischen

T +352 (0)48 39 68

www.intempo.lu

info@intempo.lu

A COUNTRY HOUSE
IN THE KEMPEN WOODLAND

D ankers Decor is one of the most important painting companies in the Benelux, with contracts in New York, USA, Hong Kong, the United Arab Emirates, etc.

Eddy Dankers, business manager of the company, works closely together with the renowned antiquarian Axel Vervoordt on a lot of projects: for instance he realized all the paintwork in the Chateau of 's-Graven-wezel and Kanaal, both of Axel Vervoordt.
A lot of colours and pigments were created especially for the antiquarian.

Axel Vervoordt also advised Eddy Dankers for the interior of his own home in the Kempen. This report illustrates the result of their constant search for perfection, not only in the use of colours and painting techniques (e.g. with Corical paints from Arte Constructo), but also in the choice of antique objects and furniture (from Axel Vervoordt) and the soft furnishings with fabrics from Vera Dankers (Dankers Creation).

Woodwork from Axel Vervoordt in Eddy Dankers' office.

In the night landing there is an exceptional sculpture from the antiquarian Vervoordt. The curtain decoration was provided by Dankers Creation, the company of Vera Dankers. All the walls were finished in lime based paints.

68-69
The kitchen was painted with lime based paints in light colours. The monastery table is from Axel Vervoordt. The small 18th century wall tiles are a combination of "peacock tails" and manganese.

70-71
The walls of the orangery were finished with lime wash to obtain a weathered effect. The monolithic "Pastelone" floor is a combination of brick dust and chalk: a process that is extremely labour intensive but gives a fabulous result.

[**Dankers Decor bvba**
  Painting company
  Nonnenstraat 36
  B – 2560 Nijlen
  T +32 (0)3 411 19 21
  www.dankers.be
  info@dankers.be

[**Dankers Creation bvba**
  Curtain decoration and fabrics
  Statieplein 3
  B – 2560 Nijlen
  T +32 (0)3 481 84 54
  F +32 (0)3 411 01 40
  MOB +32 (0)476 293 448 (Vera Dankers)
  info@dankerscreation.be

[**Axel Vervoordt**
  Antiques
  www.axel-vervoordt.com

[**Arte Constructo bvba**
  Traditional lime based paints
  www.arteconstructo.be

TRADITIONAL CRAFTSMANSHIP
AND FEELING FOR HARMONY

The family company Lefèvre Interiors has been giving the interior of many homes a soul since 1890. Impassioned professionals from their own ateliers bring an interior to life with their panellings and precision work.

The extensive professional and product knowledge of Lefèvre Interiors guarantee the unique interpretation and supervision of your modern day interior concept.

Tradition and innovation go hand in hand: years of expertise are coupled with a modern business model. Lefèvre Interiors is and remains craftsmanship, quality and mastery.

The private home of Greet Lefèvre, manageress of Lefèvre Interiors, in the Flemish Ardennes is a striking example of this craftsmanship and high-principled quality. Traditionally manufactured interior furnishing here go hand in hand with the carefully selected antique elements: ancient floors, antique furniture and objects that give the whole an authentic aura.

The hall (with a view on the library) is paved
with floor tiles in a chequered pattern,
interchanging Noir de Mazy and Carrara-
marble.
A 19th century bronze lantern.

The staircase hall with floor tiles in a chequered pattern.
The staircase is made with steps in recycled Carrara marble.
A wrought iron staircase banister as in an antique model.

The dining room is English inspired. The walls were painted with Rectory Red from Farrow & Ball. An antique English commode and curtains made in a fabric from Brunschwig & Fils. A 19th century parquet floor in Hungarian point, a made to measure door and an English mantelpiece in mahogany.

The drawing room with a central 18th century walnut mantelpiece in French Regency style with original patine and inside worked with Burgundian tiles. The oak doors were made to measure. Paintings by Jean-Marc Louis.

An antique wine table.

The furniture and panelling were made and patined in the Lefèvre Interiors ateliers.

78-79
An antique grey patined cupboard next to the mantelpiece.
The chairs were made to measure. Several works by Jean-Marc Louis.
The plank floor is covered with an antique Iranian "Birdjand" carpet.

A solid wooden library in aged oak from the Lefèvre collection fully made to measure.
19th century parquet tiles. Above the mantelpiece the painting "Le 102ᵉ Dalmatien"
by the Belgian artist Thierry Poncelet.
Right a modern work by the Belgian painter Scrivo.

83-85
The country living kitchen with cupboards in bleached oak. A French 18th century oak table and French 19th century chairs.
Floor in large recycled Carrara marble tiles. The same natural stone was used for the work top. A La Cornue cooker and Dutch "whites" as wall tiles. An antique console table with a marble top.

The orangey with oak roof tiles, a floor in recycled brick, steel windows and an antique French mantelpiece.
Above the mantelpiece a 19th century mirror in Neogothic style.

The bathroom floor is covered with
recycled Carrara marble.
The sink unit furniture and the bath
surround were made of oak and covered
with Carrara marble.

Lefèvre Interiors

Reynaertstraat 6A

B – 8710 Wielsbeke

T +32 (0)55 42 82 07

F +32 (0)56 66 57 60

www.lefevre.be

info@lefevre.be

THE WARM AND TIMELESS AURA OF CLASSIC PANELLINGS

In working out this interior concept Lefèvre Interiors took account of the client's wish to allow the various panelled rooms in this house to flow harmoniously into each other.

The choice of the interior styles and the matching colours and wood were of crucial importance in this.

The mantelpiece wall with a marble mantelpiece and a panelling in light tinted oak.

The sitting room was fully panelled in the
French Louis XVI style.
Panels in lightly tinted oak with full
integration of all hi-fi units.

A double door integrated
into the panelling with a
hand cut oak garland
above it.

This English inspired library was made in mahogany.

In the hall it was opted for wallpaper in combination with a panelling and cloakroom cupboards, all this in a sober colour pallet.

An English inspired, painted wall cupboard with low panelling in the dining room.

Lefèvre Interiors

Reynaertstraat 6A

B – 8710 Wielsbeke

T +32 (0)55 42 82 07

F +32 (0)56 66 57 60

www.lefevre.be

info@lefevre.be

[ETHNIC INSPIRATION

This timeless home surprises the visitor as soon as they enter the entrance hall because of the calm it emanates and the wealth of works of art from all the different regions.

The materials chosen, which are used consistently throughout the house, are used in perfect harmony with the modern furniture and fine floors.
The unity in the use of colours does the large collection of African and Asian its full justice.
The textiles and carpets add to the intimate, refined character of this living environment.
The rooms under the beams on the top floor are designed in a colonial style, again to emphasise the ethnic pieces.

This mix creates a perfect balance in this home designed by Yvette Feder (Fedecor bvba).

Upon entry, the sober colours of the floor in Burgundy stone and the staircase ensure that all emphasis is put on the art, here with several African masks.

The large fireplace in French stone is framed on both sides by objects from African and Asian origin.
The Thai coffee table combines well with the sofas, which are covered with a wool piqué. The oak floor links this room with the other rooms,
which have floors made from Burgundy stone.
The small living corner invites you to read in the large chairs, upholstered with velour.

The stylish kitchen with its soft colours is equipped will all modern comforts and a work surface made from granite.
In the dining room there is a table made from woven bamboo, with very comfortable and high chairs.
In the background there is a futon with a large collection of curiosities and souvenirs, brought back from many distant travels. A large cotton and linen carpet marks out this area.

The master bedroom radiates calm. The large bed is covered with a fabric made from velour. The carpet is linen and cotton.

The adjoining bathroom. The washbasin is covered in marble
mosaique with oak doors, finished with wengé.
The dressing table provides continuity in materials and colours.

The guest room under the rafters bathes in a colonial
atmosphere with its high beams.
The bed with lots of cushions is covered with cotton and linen
textiles, in perfect symbiosis with the rest of the house.

Fedecor sprl
Yvette Feder
fedecor@iway.be
M +32 (0)475 62 46 81

BETWEEN ANCIENT AND CONTEMPORARY

C hris van Eldik and Wendy Jansen opened an interior-design company about ten years ago in Wijk bij Duurstede in the Netherlands, called De Zon van Duurstede (The Sun of Duurstede). Their style can best be described as "streamlined classic": a combination of warm, natural, honest, basic materials and fabrics, but in a definitely contemporary, almost minimalist setting.

This husband-and-wife team were among the pioneers of lime paints, which have enjoyed great success in recent years. The choice of these paints is completely in keeping with their designs, which are timeless, sober and cosy, all at the same time.

Chris and Wendy also design their own furniture line under the name of JOB interiors. They started with chairs and sofas, and then went on to create a collection of refectory tables.

This report shows an architect's house in Zeeland (The Netherlands) where JOB Interieur / De Zon van Duurstede delivered all custom-made furniture, a few antique objects and furniture, and colour advice.

In the large seating corner all the seating elements were custom-made in dark grey cotton, with oak occasional tables, as well by Job Interieur.
Dark brown grey panels are used in the background that provide additional warmth and intimacy.

Two linen armchairs of the Max model and a 3.5 Huygen model couch.
The painting above the fireplace, an artwork by Christiaan Lieverse, was also supplied by Job Interieur. The stool in front of the fireplace, inspired by the 1970's, is made from snakeskin leather.

The root wood bench on the right comes from Indonesia.

Six Job 09 aubergine linen dining chairs around an oak monastery table, customer-made by Job Interieur. The antique Chinese stools on the table were also supplied by Job Interieur / De Zon van Duurstede. The painting is by Ramon Otting. Walls painted in aubergine lime-based paint, perfectly matching the chairs.

Job 09 chairs covered in rubber around a custom-made X-frame oak dining table. The antlers from the Canadian reindeer were made into a chandelier.

Two Stijn armchairs and an old jug, transformed into a lamp.
An antique French table is used as a desk, with two rubber Job 06 chairs.
To the extreme right on the right photo there is an early 19th century wardrobe in poplar wood, originating from Italy with the original patina.

A Job 09 chair covered in aubergine linen.

⌐ **De Zon van Duurstede**
  Job Interieur
  Oeverstraat 21
  NL – 3961 AM Wijk bij Duurstede
  T +31 (0)343 578818
  www.zonvanduurstede.nl
  www.jobinterieur.nl
  jobint@xs4all.nl

NEWLY BUILT
AND STILL AUTHENTIC

This beautiful country mansion with unique panoramic views is situated in the middle of meadows in the Noorderkempen near Antwerp: an exceptional project by Porte Bonheur.

By using old building materials and with an eye for detail, this house full of character has grown into a pleasant, attractive home, where sight has not been lost of modern-day living comfort.

The floor consists of old black bricks
laid on their sides.

The entrance hall.
An old pinewood door with an authentic handle.
The window is made of oak.
The old, renovated sink is operated with a foot
pump.
Old French pottery by Gonny Houtakkers
decoration.

An old terracotta floor and a miller's staircase made to measure in pinewood, which leads to the wine cellar.

Artwork from gallery Geukens & De Vil: Renaat Ivens
(white diptych and purple work).
In the library: a work by Fors (gallery Geukens & De Vil)
and old pottery by Gonny Houtakkers decoration.
The library cupboard was made to measure in old
pinewood.
An antique Kelim carpet.

116-117
The drawing room was
covered with an oak, aged
parquet floor.
A plastered open fireplace
with a small steel window to
the left.
Left a monochrome diptych
by Renaat Ivens.
An old French vase.

Whitewashed walls in warm tints were chosen everywhere.
The lamp hoods in linen were made to measure.
An old terracotta floor (red/black mixture).

A hand-made, wrought iron window with old glass (opens out).
A wrought iron door in combination with old pinewood planks and old glass.
An old, long farmers table and bench from France.
The open fireplace was plastered.
Handmade service from France and Sardinia (Gonny Houtakkers decoration). An old pinewood floor and beam.
Moroccan zelliges above the cooking zone.

The night hall was covered
with floor stucco with a
limestone basis.

Made to measure old pinewood doors with authentic handles.
The white artwork is by Renaat Ivens. A steel window and whitewashed walls.

Sand-coloured whitewashed walls.

A staircase with old terracotta tiles.

An old "bordure de jardin".
A made to measure sink unit furniture in old pinewood.
The mirrors were bricked in.

Shower with bench and recess.

[**Porte Bonheur**

www.portebonheur.be

[**Galerie Geukens & De Vil**

www.geukensdevil.be

Gonny Houtakkers decoration:
0032 (0)475 674 425

An old red Kelim. Artwork by Renaat Ivens (red) and Keith Brumberg (3-panel). Left above a shower in black stucco with a limestone basis. A made to measure sink unit furniture in old pinewood. Right above: a shower in aubergine coloured natural stone.

TIMELESS MINIMALISM IN
A FARMHOUSE IN WEST FLANDERS

A m projects, Mark Mertens got the commission to design and complete the interior of this farmhouse in West Flanders.

Am projects were also in the running for the interior décor. The aim was a timeless, minimalist interior, which still radiated a certain warmth. Much use was made of natural materials throughout this project. Colour accents were added by the furniture and paintwork.

The entrance hall was made with recuperation terracotta floors.
The doors to the bureau and the living room were made of solid oak.

The dining area was fully panelled and painted in an aubergine tint.
A hidden door with access to the bureau was made in the panelling.

The panelling around the fireplace was made of solid oak by Am projects.
The doors are fitted with snap-locks.
Furniture from the Am projects collection covered with Belgian and Italian linen.
An antique Louis XIII bergère in walnut.

There is an antique Italian table in the dining area.

A seat from the collection of Am projects in Belgian linen in the family room.

A daybed, poof and coffee table in linen and cotton in green tints.

The kitchen was made by Am projects in solid oak and later lye washed. The blue stone was trimmed by hand. La Cornue cooker with rear wall in zelliges.

Plank wall with recessed Gaggenau refrigerator
and doors to the cellar and mudroom.

Bar stools and couch, made to measure by Am projects and covered with English linen.

Mud room with built-in oak cupboards and a
solid blue stone sink.

Office and library were made in oak. A recessed cupboard for the computer.

Bathroom in tadelakt and oak.

The bath surround was made by Am projects in solid oak.

Am Projects
Mark Mertens
Overheide 66
B – 2870 Puurs
M +32 (0)475 70 83 80
T +32 (0)3 889 46 40
F +32 (0)3 889 73 51
www.amprojects.be

[AN INTERIOR WITH A SOUL

An interior with a soul: that was the wish of the residents.
From this basis the interior architect from Vlassak-Verhulst carefully selected century's old recuperated materials and worked closely together with craftsmen who ensured a perfect integration of these historic elements in the home with contemporary home comfort.

The finishing touch was created by the subtle use of old painting techniques and the furnishing by the antiquarian Garnier.

The old walnut panelling to the left and right of the 17th century Venetian fireplace conceal the modern media equipment.

With growing children in the home the residents had more need for a family room.

The Versailles parquet was recuperated from an old chateau in Provence. The panels primarily comprise walnut with oak inlay.

154-157
The dining room was painted in a homemade lime-wash. The furniture was provided by the antiquarian Garnier.

The living kitchen with a bluestone floor in a half-stone pattern.

View from the living area.

160
The oak laundry room, with the door fittings as a unique detail.

Ceiling high cupboards according to an
old model, with hand applied patina.

Rouge belge and white Carrara marble in a classical floor pattern.

Vlassak-Verhulst

Moerstraat 53

B – 2970 's-Gravenwezel

T +32 (0)3 658 12 50

F +32 (0)3 658 46 45

www.vlassakverhulst.be

A LOVE OF ART, ANTIQUES AND TRADITIONAL CRAFTS

The residents of this exceptional home on the Waal in Ridderkerk have a love of art and antiques and a true admiration for any authentic and handmade crafts.

The interior design fits seamlessly to the philosophy of carefully selected recuperation materials, traditional woodwork and exceptional metal fittings. To allow some art objects to come into their own even more the decision was consciously made for intense colours and special painting techniques.

The imposing entrance hall with monumental staircase. The sculpted grapevines on the pilaster are a wink at the profession of the residents.

The night landing and entrance hall with monumental staircase. The floors are covered in old marbles, the walls in traditional wood panelling.

The guest toilet with reclaimed marble.

An octagonal formal dining room, equipped all around with solid panelling, partly painted with fine floral motifs.
The left glass display cabinet conceals a walk-in tableware cupboard.

Old terracotta tiles for the floor of this lavender blue linen room.

The wall above the La Cornue stove is covered in hand-painted tiles.

View to the living kitchen.

Toile de Jouy and Carrara for the guest bathroom.

A trompe-l'oeil in this Italian inspired bathroom.

A combination of walnut and painted cupboards for the dressing room and the master bathroom. Like in all living areas special attention was also paid here to the cupboard fittings.

[**Vlassak-Verhulst**

Moerstraat 53

B – 2970 's-Gravenwezel

T +32 (0)3   658 12 50

F +32 (0)3   658 46 45

www.vlassakverhulst.be

AN EXCEPTIONAL COUNTRY HOUSE FOR PASSIONATE ANTIQUARIANS

Antiques dealer Jean-Philippe Demeyer and his colleagues, residents of the house, found this exceptional monument a few kilometers outside Bruges. It was the ideal place for them to receive customers and friends, to present antique collections and to talk about the furnishing of their homes and offices.

The walled in home dates from the 13th century and is an example of the Bruges stepped gable gothic. What started as a small medieval country house or hunting lodge had grown by 2010 into a complex of buildings from different periods, in various styles and always in different bricks.

All buildings are grouped around a double inner courtyard with pigeon loft and majestic cedar, with the exception of the orangery built in the Victorian era by an Englishman on a filled-in moat.

When they found the building it had been empty for decades, there was no electricity, heating or water. Fortunately only a few of the genuine features had been lost over the last decades due to the long vacancy.

In the first place an attempt was made in giving the building a soul again, giving back its pride by respecting it and allowing it to be what it is: a hard balancing act...

Every space was given its original function again and this proved the most natural way to inhabit the house.

This is a ten year plan for Jean-Philippe Demeyer, Frank Ver Elst and Jean-Paul Dewever, which has currently already been half-finished. Since November 2008 the antiquarian trio has been living and working in this historic property.

The oldest part of the house, entirely in water, with the old stone bridge, the Tudor gate and the carpentry have been returned to the original mustard colour.

The open entrance with large wooden gate and brick vaults, Spanish 18th century terracotta dishes and mid-European blue rustic bench.
The property has been a listed monument since 1964.

The library with an exceptional coloured Chinese carpet (c. 1940) and English easy chairs in harmony with the colours of the carpet.
The walls are painted in the same duck-egg green and then polished.

The Chinese drawing room with turquoise velvet chairs
from the 1940's and a 1970 red lacquered table and English
arts and crafts, a Chinese inspired hanging light.
A white woolen long-haired 1970 carpet and Napoleon III
papier maché. A China club standing light.
The walls are painted terracotta and then polished.

The office with white painted neogothic cupboards and turquoise floor lamp on the table. The walls are painted grass green.

The kitchen with the Medieval Tudor arched chimney breast and Aga stove.
The floor is covered in Flemish blue terracotta and the walls and beams are repainted in the original colours.
A large English bacon-settee is placed by the kitchen table.
The hall is also used as a dining room in the winter by the large Gothic Flemish chimney.
The walls are painted in a diamond point pattern.
The 18th century table is from Switzerland.
The old wooden spiral staircase stands in the corner of the room.

The carriage house with old looseboxes.
The room with the boxes was painted pink and the boxes themselves khaki as an alternative for the obligate black.

Goods are stored in these rooms.

The bathroom is bright blue with the central bath in front of the old mantelpiece.

The orangery was lime-washed again in the original
ochre yellow.
This orangery is used for parties in the summer and to
overwinter plants that need it in the winter.
The iron windows have a unique wheel system at the
top of each window to allow them to slide open.
They are original and were restored and repainted in
"Laken greenhouse- green".

Jean-Philippe Demeyer
Frank Ver Elst
Jean-Paul Dewever

« rooigem »

B – 8310 brugge

www.rooigem.com

Shop open at weekends:

Sparrendreef 98

B – 8300 Knokke

[ADDRESSES]

192-194
An In Tempo by Luc Leroi project.

AM Projects
Mark Mertens
Overheide 66
B – 2870 Puurs
M +32 (0)475 70 83 80
T +32 (0)3 889 46 40
F +32 (0)3 889 73 51
www.amprojects.be
P. 130-149

Arte Constructo bvba
Traditional lime based paints
www.arteconstructo.be
P. 58-73

Axel Vervoordt
Antiques
www.axel-vervoordt.com
P. 58-73

Dankers Decor bvba
Painting company
Nonnenstraat 36
B – 2560 Nijlen
T +32 (0)3 411 19 21
www.dankers.be
info@dankers.be
P. 58-73

Dankers Creation bvba
Curtain decoration and fabrics
Statieplein 3
B – 2560 Nijlen
T +32 (0)3 481 84 54
F +32 (0)3 411 01 40
MOB +32 (0)476 293 448 (Vera Dankers)
info@dankerscreation.be
P. 58-73

De Zon van Duurstede
Job Interieur
Oeverstraat 21
NL – 3961 AM Wijk bij Duurstede
T +31 (0)343 578818
www.zonvanduurstede.nl
www.jobinterieur.nl
jobint@xs4all.nl
P.98-109

Jean-Philippe Demeyer
Frank Ver Elst
Jean-Paul Dewever
« rooigem »
B – 8310 brugge
www.rooigem.com
Shop open at weekends:
Sparrendreef 98
B – 8300 Knokke
P. 176-189

Fedecor sprl
Yvette Feder
fedecor@iway.be
M +32 (0)475 62 46 81
P. 92-97

In Tempo by Luc Leroi
13a rue de Clairefontaine
L – 8460 Eischen
T +352 (0)48 39 68
www.intempo.lu
info@intempo.lu
P.16-41, 42-57

Lefèvre Interiors
Reynaertstraat 6A
B – 8710 Wielsbeke
T +32 (0)55 42 82 07
F +32 (0)56 66 57 60
www.lefevre.be
info@lefevre.be
P. 74-87, 88-91

Porte Bonheur
www.portebonheur.be
Galerie Geukens & De Vil
www.geukensdevil.be
Gonny Houtakkers decoration:
0032 (0)475 674 425
P. 110-129

Vlassak-Verhulst
Moerstraat 53
B – 2970 's-Gravenwezel
T +32 (0)3 658 12 50
F +32 (0)3 658 46 45
www.vlassakverhulst.be
P. 150-165, 166-175

PUBLISHER
BETA-PLUS Publishing
Termuninck 3
B - 7850 Edingen
www.betaplus.com
info@betaplus.com

PHOTOGRAPHY
All pictures: Jo Pauwels

GRAPHIC DESIGN
POLYDEM
Nathalie Binart

TRANSLATION
Txt-Ibis

April 2010
ISBN 13: 978-90-8944-069-3